# Days to
# Remember

By Robert Gott

CELEBRATION PRESS
Pearson Learning Group

W9-AJP-625

# Contents

# National Holidays

People celebrate national holidays all around the world. National holidays help people remember important events in the history of a country. They honor people who made that country a better place in which to live. Each national holiday has a story behind it. Let's read four of these stories.

ANZAC Day parade in Australia

# Bastille Day

## July 14

The story of Bastille Day began in France more than 200 years ago. In those days, France was ruled by King Louis XVI. The king was wealthy and enjoyed spending money. To become wealthier, he made the people of France pay high taxes to the government.

The people did not like how the king spent their taxes. Many of them were poor and could not even buy food. Those who refused to pay the taxes were sent to prison. The most famous prison was the Bastille in Paris.

**France**

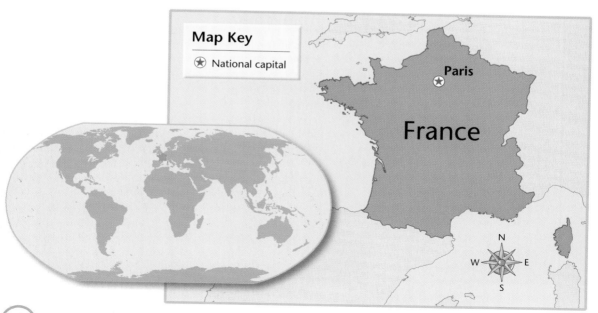

**Map Key**

⊛ National capital

Paris

France

N W E S

After some time, the people joined together to fight the king and his laws. They planned to take over the Bastille because it was a symbol of the king's power. It reminded them of what could happen if they did not obey the king. On July 14, 1789, a large group of people forced their way into the Bastille and freed the prisoners.

Louis XVI was king of France from 1774 to 1792.

Two days after the Bastille was captured, it was burned down and destroyed.

5

Airplanes fly over Paris. The planes' smoke trails are the colors of the French flag.

People crowd the streets to watch a Bastille Day parade.

This event was the beginning of the French Revolution. The revolution helped bring a new way of life for the people of France. In 1792, France became a republic. The country was ruled by its people instead of a king or queen.

Today, the people of France celebrate Bastille Day on July 14. They enjoy concerts, parades, and fireworks. This holiday reminds the people of their freedom and their rights.

# Canada Day

## July 1

The story of Canada Day began in the 1800s. At that time, Great Britain ruled much of the land now known as Canada. Canada was made up of several colonies. People in these colonies wanted to form one country separate from Great Britain. They felt it would be easier to trade their goods and to farm the land if they joined together.

Today, Canada is divided into provinces and territories.

In 1864, people from some of the colonies began meeting together. They discussed how they could form their own government. The joining of the colonies was called Canadian Confederation.

The British government agreed to the colonies' plan. On July 1, 1867, the colonies became a country called the Dominion of Canada. These colonies became the provinces of Nova Scotia, New Brunswick, Quebec, and Ontario. Canada grew larger over the next hundred years. Today, Canada has ten provinces and three territories.

◄ The Canadian colonists met in London, Great Britain, to discuss uniting the provinces.

British Columbia was a British colony ► on the west coast. It agreed to join the Dominion of Canada if a railway was built to connect it to the rest of the country. The Canadian Pacific Railway was opened in 1886.

The Canadian flag
features a maple leaf.

Canada Day is celebrated on July 1 all across the country. There are concerts, fireworks, and local events. Canada Day doesn't only celebrate Canadian Confederation. It also celebrates Canada's Aboriginal peoples. Aboriginal peoples lived in Canada for thousands of years before other groups of people arrived. They were not included in the original planning of the new country. Today, Canada Day honors them, too.

Fireworks celebrations
in Ottawa, Ontario

# ANZAC Day

## April 25

ANZAC Day is celebrated in Australia and New Zealand. ANZAC stands for the Australian and New Zealand Army Corps. The story of ANZAC Day began during World War I. In 1914, a war began in Europe. Groups of countries were fighting each other. One group was called the Allies. The other group formed the Central Powers. Australia and New Zealand sent soldiers to Europe and the Middle East as part of the Allied forces. These soldiers became known as ANZACs.

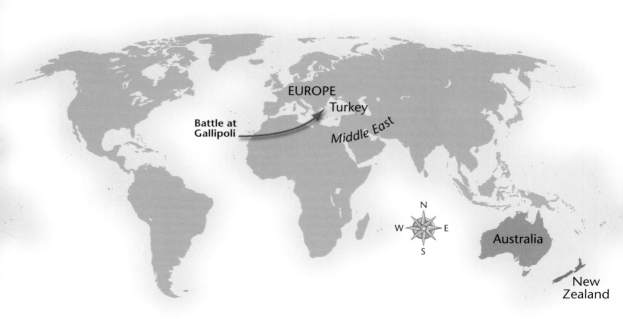

The ANZAC soldiers traveled far from Australia and New Zealand to fight with the Allies in Europe and the Middle East.

Thousands of ANZAC troops landed at the Ari Burnu beach in Gallipoli on April 25, 1915.

Some ANZAC soldiers were sent to fight in Gallipoli (guh-LIP-puh-lee), Turkey. At this time, Turkey was one of the Central Powers. On April 25, 1915, the ANZAC soldiers arrived in Gallipoli to fight the Turkish soldiers. Many ANZAC soldiers were killed as they landed on the peninsula. The soldiers fought under terrible conditions for eight months.

Jack Simpson Kirkpatrick was honored for his work in carrying wounded soldiers out of battle on his donkey, Duffy.

On April 25, people in Australia and New Zealand remember the ANZAC soldiers. ANZAC Day services are held in cities and towns all over Australia and New Zealand. People remember how hard and bravely the ANZAC soldiers fought. They also remember the men and women who fought in other wars, such as World War II, the Korean War, and Vietnam. Parades and picnics honor all of these heroic men and women.

Flowers are placed on memorials in memory of the Gallipoli soldiers.

Children honor their nation's heroes.

# Martin Luther King, Jr. Day

## Third Monday in January

**Martin Luther King, Jr.**

On the third Monday in January, people in the United States honor Martin Luther King, Jr. He was born in Atlanta, Georgia, in 1929. At that time, many states had laws that separated African Americans and white people. They couldn't eat in the same restaurants. They had separate water fountains, restrooms, and schools. If a bus was crowded, African Americans had to give up their seats to white people.

**United States of America**

United States

Atlanta
Georgia

**Map Key**
◉ City

N
W E
S

Martin Luther King, Jr. was a powerful speaker.

King tried to change the unfair laws. In 1955, a woman named Rosa Parks was arrested because she didn't give her bus seat to a white person. King helped organize a peaceful protest among African Americans. They stopped traveling by bus until the law was changed.

King organized and led more protests. On August 28, 1963, he led the famous March on Washington. It was the largest march for equal rights in history.

Rosa Parks inspired other peaceful protests with her actions. ▶

◀ Rosa Parks today

Some people fought against King and others who worked for equal rights. King was arrested and threatened, but he never gave up. Tragically, he was shot and killed in 1968.

King dreamed of a world where everyone is treated fairly and equally. His dream lived on after his death. In 1986, the first official Martin Luther King, Jr. Day was held. Schools and businesses now close all across the United States. There are services to remember King's life and his dream. People also remember those who are still working for peace.

Many streets, schools, and public buildings are named after King.

Today, children of all races learn and play together.

# Index